Other giftbooks by Helen Exley:
Our Love Story
Thinking of You
Missing You...

True Love...
Love A Celebration
A Token of Love

EDITED BY HELEN EXLEY
BORDER ILLUSTRATIONS BY SHARON BASSIN

Published simultaneously in 1997 by Exley Publications LLC in the USA, and Exley Publications Ltd in Great Britain.

12 11 10 9 8 7 6 5 4 3 2 1

Pictures researched by Image Select International.
Typeset by Delta, Watford.
Printed and bound in Spain.
Exley Publications Ltd, 16 Chalk Hill, Watford, Herts WD1 4BN, UK.
Exley Publications LLC, 232 Madison Avenue, Suite 1206, NY 10016, USA.

Acknowledgements: The publishers are grateful for permission to reproduce copyright material. Whilst every effort has been made to trace copyright holders, the publishers would be pleased to hear from any not here acknowledged. Duff Cooper: *A Durable Fire: The Letters of Duff and Diana Cooper*, ed. Artemis Cooper, HarperCollins Publisher, 1983. © Artemis Cooper. Winston Churchill: Letter to Clementine Churchill, September 1919, reproduced with permission of Curtis Brown Ltd, London on behalf of The Estate of Sir Winston Churchill. © Winston S Churchill. Zelda Fitzgerald: *Zelda Fitzgerald* by Nancy Milford, published by Bodley Head, reprinted by permission of Laurence Pollinger Ltd on behalf of the Estate of Zelda Fitzgerald. David Lloyd George: *My Darling Pussy*, ed. A.J.P. Taylor, published by Weidenfeld and Nicholson Ltd, The Orion Publishing Group. Edna Golan: *Since You Went Away*, ed. Judy Barrett Litoff & David C. Smith, © 1991 Judy Barrett Litoff & David C. Smith published by OUP, N.Y. Margaret Lawrence: *Love Letters to Baruch* by Margaret Lawrence Greene, Musson Book Company, Toronto, 1973 B.M Greene. George Bernard Shaw: *Bernard Shaw & Mrs Patrick Campbell: Their Correspondence*, published by Victor Gollancz. Edith Sokol: *Since You Went Away* ed. Judy Barnett Litoff & David Smith, © 1991 OUP, N.Y. Dylan Thomas: *The Collected Letters of Dylan Thomas*, ed. Paul Ferris, J.M. Dent & Co and Macmillan USA. Reprinted courtesy of David Higham Associates and New Directions Publishing Corp. N.Y. Letters © 1957, 1966, 1985 The Trustees for the Copyrights of Dylan Thomas. Watanabe: *Love Letters of a Japanese*, by G.N Mortlake, Stanley Paul & Co 1959.
Picture credits: Exley Publications is very grateful to the following individuals and organizations for permission to reproduce their pictures: Archiv Für Kunst (AKG), Art Resource (AR), The Bridgeman Art Library (BAL), Fine Art Photographic Library (FAP), Giraudon (GIR). p 7: John Callcott Horsley, *Madame Se Chauffe*, FAP; p 8: Besnard, *The Eclipse*, GIR/AR; p 13: © 1997 Konstantin Korowin, *Atelierszene*, AKG; p 19: Isaac Snowman, *A Letter of Love*, BAL; p 23: William Mulready, *The Sonnet*, BAL; p 28: Paul Merwart, *Portrait of Thomas Lemas*, BAL; p 33: Georg Friedrich Kersting, *Die Stickerin*, AKG; p 36: Carl Holsoe, *Girl reading in an interior*, BAL; p 40: Georgina M. de l'Aubiniere, *Fond Memories*, BAL; p 45: © 1997 Sir Walter Russell, *Marion*, BAL; p 46: John William Godward, *Dolce Far Niente*, BAL; p 50: Jean Raoux, *Young woman reading a letter*, GIR/AR; p 58/59: © 1997 Bill Brauer.

Love Letters

A HELEN EXLEY GIFTBOOK

EXLEY
NEW YORK • WATFORD, UK

*I woke up
with you in my breast
and on my lips.
Jack, I love you terribly today.
The whole world is gone.
There is only you.
I walk about, dress,
eat, write —
but all the time
I am breathing you.*

KATHERINE MANSFIELD
(1888-1923)
TO JOHN MIDDLETON MURRY

*M*e Love:

Can you feel the brilliant sunshine on this page?
And the peace? And hear the splashings of the
summer? And the laughter of the children?
And the hardness of this seat in this anchored
row boat? And see the trees and the clouds reflected
in this lake of fresh water? And see the goldenrods,
and the lovely bushes and trees all along the edge
of the water?... My darling, I need you much more
to tune me in than I need for any radio,
and I always will....
Yannie, I love thee, and always will.
Your Bee, Edna.

EDNA GOLAN
TO HER HUSBAND JOHN

THERE IS NO GRIEF, NO SORROW,

NO DESPAIR, NO LANGUOR,

NO DEJECTION, NO DISMAY,

NO ABSENCE SCARCELY CAN THERE BE,

FOR THOSE WHO LOVE AS WE DO.

WILLIAM WORDSWORTH
(1770-1850)

*W*hen I close my eyes I think that you
stand in front of me, just as when we are first
quite alone after a long separation,
and have not yet kissed each other,
but stand and feel our breaths, and bodies
quietly touch each other, and feel beforehand
the kiss coming, and the whole world seems
full of cream, jam and dizzyness.

PERCY GRAINGER

I love the scent of your hair —
I love to touch it with my lips and feel it
upon my face. See, I kiss it here
on the moonbeam that marks its parting:
and I lay my face into its coiled masses
as one might smell a mass
of clustered violets.

ROBERT BURDETTE
TO HIS FUTURE WIFE CLARA

*The sun cannot shine
without you,
the birds can
make no melody.
The flowers have
no other beauty
or perfume —
all is a
meaningless waste.
I love you darling....
You are in
every thought,
dream, hope, desire.*

AUSTIN DICKINSON
(1829-1995)
TO MABEL TODD

Sweetest Fanny,

You are always new. The last of your kisses was ever the sweetest; the last smile the brightest; the last movement the gracefullest. When you pass'd my window home yesterday, I was fill'd with as much admiration as if I had then seen you for the first time. You uttered a half complaint once that I only lov'd your Beauty. Have I nothing else then to love in you but that? Do I not see a heart naturally furnish'd with wings imprison itself with me? No ill prospect has been able to turn your thoughts a moment from me. This perhaps should be as much a subject of sorrow as joy — but I will not talk of that. Even if you did not love me I could not help an entire devotion to you: how much more deeply then must I feel for you

knowing you love me. My Mind has been the most

discontented and restless one that ever was put into a body

too small for it. I never felt my Mind repose upon

anything with complete and undistracted enjoyment —

upon no person but you. When you are in the room my

thoughts never fly out of the window: you always

concentrate my whole senses.

JOHN KEATS (1795-1821)
TO FANNY BRAWNE

*H*owever, when every morning I wake up, I look for you, it seems to me that half of myself is missing.... When I go to bed, I do not fail to make room for you; I push myself quite close to the wall and leave a great empty space in my small bed. This movement is mechanical, these thoughts are involuntary.

HONORÉ-GABRIEL RIQUETTI
TO SOPHIA RUFFEY

Everything reminds me of you so much. If I go into the drawing-room, the piano reminds me of you and your violin and the "Shepherds Dance", and "One More", and I feel miserable. Then if I go into the dining-room, there's somebody missing from the table and I'm miserable....

UNKNOWN AUTHOR
TO MARY CARTLAND (1879-1976

*F*ill your paper

with the breathings

of your heart....

WILLIAM WORDSWORTH

TO HIS WIFE MARY

My darling,
This is to warn you at the earliest possible moment
that I have once more fallen desperately in love
with an absolutely new girl. *She is the darlingest girl*
I ever met. I saw her for the first time yesterday afternoon
lying (in the most seductive attitude) on a sofa.
She was attired in a love of a dressing-gown.
She had the dearest face I ever saw —
the most alluring smile — her neck was simply provoking.
Altogether I am clean gone....
Ever and Ever Her lover.

DAVID LLOYD GEORGE (1863-1945)
TO FRANCES STEVENSON

...So if you are idly curious as to whether I am still in love with Stella, the answer is yes yes yes yes yes yes yes yes yes yes yes yes yes yes yes yes yes yes yes yes yes yes yes yes yes yes and a million times yes....

Cannot help it. Am quite sensible, quite able, quite myself, and yet a lad playing with you on the mountains and unable to feel where you begin and I leave off. And if you tell me that you feel like that the sky will not be high enough for me (isn't that a nice Irish phrase?) Heavens! how delicious it is to make love to you!!!!!

G.B.S.

GEORGE BERNARD SHAW
(1856-1950)
TO "STELLA", BEATRICE CAMPBELL

Tonight we would have walked together, arm in arm,
for it is a clear moonlit night, one of those nights made
for lovers. And you would have your hand in my pocket
to keep it warm. Oh, Glad; sweetheart, if I could
honourably come to you now I would show you
how much I need you, how much I want to be near you.
Perhaps you think I enjoy this hell, but truly, angel,
there is hardly a moment of goodness
in my Army life so far.
Just you, you are what I want, and so long as I am
unable to be with you, I can find only a fraction of light
in my world. Whatever comes to try and part us
will lose the fight against our perfect love,
Glad.... Keep lovely and wonderful always
for Your Gill.

GILBERT (GILL) MUDIE
TO GLADYS TOOKER

I was at your house tonight. They showed me some
pictures of you taken in your high school class room
and track team. The one I liked best was the one
where you and another fellow were ready to start running.
I looked at you,
and this is what went thru my mind.
That hair is cropped close, but still is curled around
my finger as if it were grasping it. I've kissed those lips.
That expression I've seen so often. These legs
were pressed against mine. I've held those wrists
with my fingers. My hands have been in those hands.
My fingers have touched those sides and both
touched lightly and dug into those shoulders.
My lips have kissed that throat.
And I know you had to be alive because you're

so alive! Do you know what I mean?... Darling,
come to me in a dream tonight and tell me that
you're alive and safe. Please! I know you want
to tell me. Maybe somewhere in a prison camp
tonight you're
saying to yourself that tonight you're going to try
to tell me that you're alive. If there's anything good
in the world, they'll let you tell me.
Now to sleep, and to wait for your message.
I'll love you till I die.
Myra.

MYRA A. STRACHNER, TO PRIVATE BERNIE
STALLER, WHO HAD BEEN REPORTED AS MISSING
IN ACTION. ON MARCH 18, 1945, THE DAY AFTER
MYRA WROTE THIS LETTER, BERNIE WAS KILLED
IN ACTION.

$\mathcal{I}$ MY DARLING BILL,

want you to realise what a tremendous difference you make to my life. Days are so much happier because of the wonder of you and your love. Somehow I have felt it — inadequate — to take out a pad and write to you. What is there new to say? Each day, the wonder of love and joy is renewed when I realise that the world has you in it.

It is Sunday and the fire is blazing in a Christmassy way. It reminds me of a night when we put out the light and sat by the fire. It was painful to be so close to you in those days... but then so wonderful to discover that we felt the same about each other.

I didn't really love you in those days, like I do now... I was still a kid and didn't know what it was to love so much that it tore at one's insides to see the door shutting on one's dream man. It was not long before you taught me, not only love for you, but utter givingness to others.

It radiates from you all the time.

It sounds as though I found it tough falling in love. It was so difficult not to. I suppose women don't usually blather like this to their men folk, but I can't bear your not knowing that you mean more to me than anything or anyone. More even than bananas! Rough seas and stormy skies, miles of land and water cannot cut us off from each other. One day, the bells will ring again and it will be my happiest day. I belong to you. All my love, Helen.

HELEN TO BILL COOK.
IN 1942 BILL WENT TO WAR FOR
OVER FOUR YEARS,
AND WHILE HE WAS AWAY THEY
EXCHANGED 6000 LETTERS

I am writing to you on Sunday evening, which

is the time I like to write to you best, because

I feel the quietest and descend the most into my real

self, where my love is strongest and deepest.

So you know I always have a fancy at such times

that our love makes us somehow alone together in

the world. We seem to have a deep life together

apart from all other people on earth, and

which we cannot show, explain or impart to them.

At least my affection seems to isolate me in

the deepest moments from all others, and it

makes me speak with my whole heart and soul

to you and you only.

WALTER BAGEHOT
TO ELIZA WILSON,
1858

*But do you know what it is to wait
five months for a kiss?
Do you know what a poor heart endures,
that for five months has felt, day by day,
hour by hour, life abandon it,
the cold of the tomb descend slowly
in the solitude, death and oblivion
falling drop by drop like snow?*

ALFRED DE MUSSET
TO GEORGE SAND
(AURORE DUDEVANT)

... and remember, each moment
I am robbed of you, each night and all nights
I am turned away from you, turned out by you,
give me pangs
the exquisiteness of which must be measured
by the knowledge that they are moments
and nights
lost, lost, lost forever.

JACK LONDON (1876-1916)
TO HIS FUTURE WIFE
CHARMIAN KITTERIDGE

Goody, Goody, dear Goody,

You said you would weary and I do hope in my heart you are wearying. It will be so sweet to make it all up to you in kisses when I return. You will take me and hear all my bits of experiences, and your heart will beat when you find how I have longed to return to you....

Darling, Dearest, Loveliest, "The Lord bless you". I think of you every hour, every moment. I love you and admire you, like – like anything.

My own Good Good!

Good night, my beloved. Dream of me.

I am ever

Your own

GOODY.

JANE CARLYLE (1801-1866)
TO THOMAS CARLYLE

I look down the tracks and see you coming — and out of every haze & mist your darling rumpled trousers are hurrying to me — Without you, dearest dearest I couldn't see or hear or feel or think — or live — I love you so and I'm never in all our lives going to let us be apart another night. It's like begging for mercy of a storm or killing Beauty or growing old, without you. I want to kiss you so — and in the back where your dear hair starts and your chest — I love you — and I can't tell you how much — To think that I'll die without your knowing — Goofo, you've got to try [to] feel how much I do —

how inanimate I am when you're gone —
I can't even hate these damnable people —
Nobody's got any right to live but us —
and they're dirtying up our world
and I can't hate them because I want you so
— Come Quick — Come Quick to me —
I could never do without you
if you hated me and were covered with sores
like a leper — if you ran away with another
woman and starved me and beat me —
I still would want you I know....

ZELDA FITZGERALD
(1900-1948)
TO F. SCOTT FITZGERALD

... darling, how I love you!...
I thought last night I might be able
to drown myself in sleep.
But divil a bit, fearfully restless
with a sort of feeling of regret and pain —
up and down my room I had to walk
like a caged animal,
and indeed I'm no better in the daytime.
I wrote two letters last night to you
and burnt them both.
I'm shivering so that I can't write....

UNKNOWN AUTHOR
TO
MARY CARTLAND
(1879-1976)

$\mathscr{C}$ruel stony hearted wretch, snatcher of bread
from a starving child, how had you the heart?
how could you? do you know what it means to me?
I want my plaything that I am to throw away.
I want my Virgin Mother enthroned in heaven.
I want my Italian peasant woman....
I want my rapscallionly fellow vagabond.
I want my dark lady. I want my angel —
I want my tempter. I want my Freia with
her apples. I want the lighter of my seven lamps
of beauty, honour, laughter, music, love, life
and immortality....
I want my inspiration, my folly, my happiness,

my divinity, my madness, my selfishness,

my final sanity and sanctification, my

transfiguration, my purification,

my light across the sea, my palm across

the desert, my garden of lovely flowers,

my million nameless joys, my day's wage,

my night's dream, my darling and my star....

O cruel, cruel, cruel, cruel, have you

no heart at all?

G.B.S.

GEORGE BERNARD SHAW
(1856-1950)
TO
"STELLA", BEATRICE CAMPBELL

But your belongings are like that for me —
they're sacred. When I see your hat, it becomes
"the only hat in the world" for me.
Do you know how I love you, you strange
little husband? Do you know how I dream
sometimes that your darling dark head is
beside me on the pillows?... how often
I have just touched you, sleeping, with
my hand — or watched that dark beloved
boyish head turned away from me?

KATHERINE MANSFIELD
(1888-1923)
TO JOHN MIDDLETON MURRY

Caitlin. Just to write down your name like
*that. **Caitlin.** I don't have to say My dear,*
My darling, my sweetheart, though I do
say those words, to you in myself, all day
and night. Caitlin. And all the words
are in that one word. Caitlin, Caitlin,
and I can see your blue eyes and your golden
hair and your slow smile and your faraway
voice. Your faraway voice is saying, now,
at my ear, the words you said in your
last letter, and thank you, dear, for the
love you said and sent. I love you.
Never forget that, for one single moment
of the long, slow, sad Laugharne day,
never forget it in your mazed trances, in
your womb & your bones, in our bed at night.
I love you. Over this continent I take

your love inside me, your love goes with

me up in the aeroplaned air, into all the

hotel bedrooms where momentarily

I open my bag — half full, as ever, of dirty shirts

— and lay down my head & do not sleep until

dawn because I can hear your heart beat beside

me, your voice saying my name and our love

above the noise of the night-traffic, above the

neon flashing, deep in my loneliness, my love.

DYLAN THOMAS
(1914-1953)
TO HIS WIFE
CAITLIN

When you come back, there are so many things
I want to do together. Although I want to settle down,
and although there's a whole future together to plan,
I still want to do the little ordinary things I've missed
doing with you in the past fourteen months! I want to
smile at you across the table at the Statler's;
I want to hold your hand at the Playhouse and the Hanna;
I want to walk proudly down the aisle with you
to the dress circle at the Music Hall; I want you
to watch me try on dresses at Halle's; I want to stroll
down Euclid Ave. with you; I want to love you madly
each night; I want you to meet every child in the school;
I want to ride with you in the morning sunlight past
Shaker Lakes; I want to take a shower with you;
I want you to kiss me good-morning and good-night;
I want to watch you shave. Oh darling — I want you
so very much!! I love you more than I can ever put into
words — I wish my heart could spill love on you,
like my mouth can water yours with kisses!
All my love ever and ever,
Edith.

EDITH SOKOL
TO
HER HUSBAND VICTOR

SCOTT —

there's nothing in all the world I want but you — and your
precious love — All the material things
are nothing. I'd just hate to live a sordid, colorless existence —
because you'd soon love me less —
and less — and I'd do anything — anything — to keep your
heart for my own — I don't want to live —
I want to love first, and live incidentally — Why don't you feel
that I'm waiting — I'll come to you, Lover, when you're ready
— Don't — don't ever think of
the things you can't give me — You've trusted me
with the dearest heart of all — and it's so
damn much more than anybody else in all the world has ever
had —

How can you think deliberately of life without me — If you should die — O Darling — darling Scott — It'd be like going blind. I know I would, too, — I'd have no purpose in life — just a pretty — decoration.
Don't you think I was made for you?
I feel like you had me ordered — and I was delivered to you — to be worn — I want you to wear me, like a watch — charm or a button hole bouquet — to the world. And then, when we're alone, I want to help — to know that you can't do anything without me.

ZELDA FITZGERALD (1900-1948)
TO F. SCOTT FITZGERALD

LONG LOVE

*I was never so miserable at leaving you
as tonight, not even that first time when
I left you in New York....
We have been so very much together
these last ten days, and so wonderfully happy.
In all our twelve years of marriage,
I do not think there has been anything
to equal it.
You grow always not only dearer to me
but more necessary, and you become
all the time better, wiser and more
to be adored.*

DUFF COOPER
TO
DIANA

*M*y darling one

Only these few lines to mark the eleventh time
we have seen the 12th Sept. together.
How I rejoice to think of my gt good fortune
on that day! There came to me the greatest happiness
and the greatest honour of my life....
My dear it is a rock of comfort to have yr love
and companionship at my side.
Every year we have formed more bonds
of deep affection....
I can never express my gratitude to you
for all you have done for me and for all
you have been to me.
Yr ever loving and devoted
W.

WINSTON CHURCHILL (1874-1965)
TO CLEMENTINE

A letter from you,

and the universe

(that's me) sings.

MALCOLM LOWRY

TO

JAN GABRIAL

GOOD MORNING

Though still in bed my thoughts go out to you,

my Immortal Beloved, now and then joyfully,

then sadly, waiting to learn whether or not fate

will hear us. I can live only wholly with you

or not at all — yes, I am resolved to wander

so long away from you until I can fly to

your arms and say that I am really at home,

send my soul enwrapped in you into the

land of spirits. Yes, unhappily it must be so —

you will be the more resolved since you know

my fidelity — to you, no one can ever again

possess my heart — none — never — Oh, God!

why is it necessary to part from one whom one

so loves and yet my life in W. [Vienna]

is now a wretched life — your love makes me

at once the happiest and the unhappiest of men —

at my age, I need a steady, quiet life —

can that be under our conditions?... Be calm,

only by a calm consideration of our existence

can we achieve our purpose to live together –

be calm – love me – today – yesterday –

what tearful longings for you – you – you –

my life – my all – farewell –

Oh, continue to love me – never misjudge

the most faithful heart of your beloved L.

ever thine

ever mine

ever for each other.

LUDWIG VAN BEETHOVEN

(1770-1827)

TO HIS "IMMORTAL BELOVED"

*All my thoughts
are concentrated
in your boudoir,
in your bed,
on your heart.*

NAPOLEON BONAPARTE
(1769-1821)
TO HIS WIFE JOSEPHINE

*Oh, my heart
is thirsty for
your kisses....*

NATHANIEL HAWTHORNE
TO SOPHIA PEABODY

I think that never in a thousand letters

could I ever begin to tell you what it means

to me to be able to come home to you.

I never realized how starved I was

for this deep wonderful sweetness, a small place

where my love lives which he gives to me

as my own, and tells me is mine.

It's a symbol of the sweetness and the peace

I know with you.

It's made up of all our hours together — the hours

of the days and nights we have had together.

It means music to me, and the blessing of good food,

preparing it for you and me to eat together.

It means the talking one can only do with one's

dearest, closest, oldest friend and the silences one

falls into only with this friend. It means all

the happy things done together, and work that

suddenly became play because it has been shared

with a friend and a lover.

MARGARET LAWRENCE TO BENEDICT GREENE

Heart of my heart — I am sitting on pebbles by the sea shore three hours from Tokio.... The waves approach me and retire; when it approaches it brings their sweet message from you, and when it retires it brings my message to you. The waves move to and fro from me and from you. The wave swells like the pulse of our love, and it sweeps suddenly very big — seemingly without cause, just as it is so with our love.

KENRIO WATANABE
TO MERTYL MEREDITH

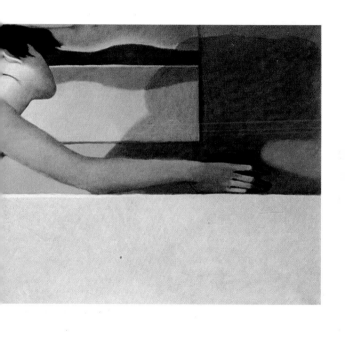

*T*he Shortest and Sweetest of Songs

Come

Home.

GEORGE MacDONALD

(1824-1905)

When you have gone away,
No flowers more, methinks, will be —
No maple leaves in all the world —
Till you come back to me.

YANAGIWARA YASU-KO
(1783-1866)